All About Steph Curry

Inspiring stories, facts and trivia about basketball's greatest shooter

All the history, details and incredible feats you need to know as a superfan of Steph Curry

ColorCraftBooks.com

Table Of Contents

Claim Your Free Bonus Coloring Book

There's a free bonus coloring book download waiting for you, as a thank you for picking up this book. We think you'll like it.

Just scan the QR code below or visit
ColorCraftBooks.com/colorcraft-bonus.

Kids: Make sure to ask a parent first!

Scan to get your free coloring book download:

Introduction: The Incredible Shot

Imagine being at a basketball game: the stadium is packed, the crowd is loud, and everyone is on the edge of their seats. The game clock is ticking down, and Stephen Curry, famous for his shooting, has the ball.

With only seconds left, he takes a long shot from behind the three-point line. The ball flies through the air and goes straight into the basket as the buzzer sounds. The crowd goes wild with excitement!

This amazing shot wasn't just any basket; it was a game-winning shot that helped Stephen's team, the Golden State Warriors, move forward in the playoffs. It was a moment that showed the world just how great Stephen is at basketball.

Steph didn't start out famous. He was born in Akron, Ohio, in 1988, and grew up in a family that loved sports. His dad, Dell, was a professional basketball player, and his mom, Sonya, was a college volleyball player.

With sports all around him, Stephen started playing basketball at a young age. He learned a lot from his dad and practiced all the time with his younger brother, Seth, who also became a professional basketball player.

Being a professional basketball player was Steph's dream, but it wasn't easy. He was often smaller than the other players, which made it tough for him along the way.

But Steph never gave up. He worked hard every day, practicing his shooting and playing in as many games as he could.

Steph's hard work paid off when he went to college at Davidson, where he became a star player. He led his team to many wins and broke records with his incredible shooting skills. Soon, everyone knew he was going to make it big in the NBA.

Stephen Curry's story is all about believing in yourself and working hard. It shows us that anyone can achieve their dreams with passion and dedication. No matter how tough things get, keep trying and never give up.

In this book, we'll follow Stephen's journey from a young boy with a dream to one of the best basketball players in the world. Get ready to be inspired!

Chapter 1: Splash! Meet Steph Curry, Basketball's Shooting Star

"Be the best version of yourself in anything you do. You don't have to live anybody else's story."
\- Stephen Curry

Stephen Curry's journey in basketball is an amazing story. From a young boy with big dreams in Charlotte, North Carolina, to a superstar lighting up the NBA courts, Steph has had to work hard to create his own path to success from the very beginning.

Born into a family that loved sports, Steph's early basketball knowledge came from his father, Dell Curry, who was a professional player.

Steph learned the fundamentals of basketball at a young age, practicing shots and dribbling in his backyard after school.

Unlike other kids who might have played different sports, Stephen was already focused on becoming a great basketball player.

As Steph grew, so did his understanding of the game. His father taught him basketball techniques, as well as the mental aspect of sports — staying calm under pressure, analyzing the game, and making quick decisions.

These lessons were extra important, since Steph was usually not the most physically imposing player on the team.

Some people thought he wouldn't develop into a great player, due to his smaller size. But what Step lacked in size, he more than made up for in skill, passion, and a clever basketball mind.

High school was a turning point for Steph. He played for Charlotte Christian School, where he improved his skills and began to make a name for himself.

His ability to shoot from long distance and his speed on the court started attracting attention. But it wasn't just his on-court skills that made him stand out.

His attitude and approach to the game were different to many other players. He played with joy every single game, and had a genuine love for basketball.

He would often smile, dance, and have fun during games. This made him a favorite with teammates, coaches, and fans.

College was the next big step, and even though he had success in high school, this wasn't an easy time for Steph.

He didn't receive offers from big, famous basketball colleges. He chose Davidson College, a smaller school, where he could be a leader on the team.

At this new school, Davidson, he had a big impact as soon as he started playing. He led his team to victories against much larger schools, and became famous during big tournaments like the NCAA tournament.

Did you know?

WHAT IS THE 'NCAA' TOURNAMENT?

Every year, there's a special basketball event called "March Madness," where 68 college teams play in a huge tournament. It's part of the NCAA (National Collegiate Athletic Association), which is a group for college sports in the United States. During March Madness, teams play in games in an elimination style tournament - if you lose once, you're out. This goes on until one team wins the last game and becomes the champion.

The tournament is known to be very exciting and full of surprises. Sometimes a team that nobody expects to do well suddenly wins a lot! It starts in the middle of March and finishes in early April. The games are held in different places around the country, and lots of people watch them to see new basketball stars in action.

He impressed everybody, not just due to his scoring, but also with his leadership, and the way he inspired his teammates.

Steph's time at Davidson finished with him setting scoring records and being remembered as one of the best shooters in college basketball history.

It was clear he would soon be ready for the next level—the NBA. As he entered the draft, there were still some doubts about his ability to move from college level to professional basketball, but he was used to overcoming doubts.

In the next chapter, we'll learn about Steph's start to life - where he grew up, his family, and the conditions that helped him to eventually become one of the game's greatest players ever.

Chapter 2: Little Steph: Growing Up Curry

"Success is not an accident. Success is actually a choice" - Stephen Curry

Growing up as the son of an NBA player, Stephen Curry's childhood was anything but ordinary. From a very young age, Steph was immersed in the world of professional basketball, giving him a unique point of view on the sport, and shaping his approach to the game.

Born in Akron, Ohio, but raised in Charlotte, North Carolina, USA, Steph spent many hours in basketball stadiums, watching his father, Dell Curry, play at the highest level. These times weren't just about entertainment; they were his earliest lessons in basketball.

From these games, Steph learned the rules of basketball, and also many of the more subtle parts of basketball, like mental toughness, teamwork, and strategy - which would shape his own playing style later in his career.

In addition, his mother, Sonya, was a volleyball player in college, and helped Steph understand the importance of discipline, consistency and learning. Sonya's positive attitude and supportive nature made a huge impression on Steph from a young age.

She often encouraged him to focus on the joy of the game - not just on the pressure of competition, or on winning alone.

It was about having fun first - competition and winning were secondary.

Today, we see her influence in Steph's playing style - intensely focused, and extremely skilled - but with a huge amount of joy, friendliness and sportsmanship on the court. Together, Dell and Sonya created a home life with balance.

They focused on hard work, family values, and faith. This foundation was crucial as Steph navigated the pressures and challenges of growing up in the shadow of an NBA athlete - his dad.

Steph has a younger brother, Seth, who also plays in the NBA. The two brothers regularly played on their backyard basketball court.

These friendly family games were very competitive, and were full of lessons about sportsmanship and being strong and resilient. It was here that Steph began to develop his signature playing style — quick, precise, and always with an eye for the basket.

His brother, Seth, was his biggest competitor in the early days!

Did you know?

CHEF CURRY: MASTER OF POPCORN

Steph's skills aren't limited to basketball. He's also quite the chef at home, especially known for his popcorn-making skills. Steph also loves cooking breakfast foods like pancakes and French Toast, and taking charge of the family BBQ during gatherings.

Cooking is one way Steph shows creativity and care for his family's health. It's also a great way to relax while spending time with family.

School also played a big role in Steph's development. At Charlotte Christian School, he was not only a student-athlete; he was a leader both in the classroom and on the court.

He did very well in his studies, and showed strong leadership on the basketball court, too. This earned him a lot of respect among his fellow students, as well as the teachers at the school.

His talent and hard work made him a standout on his basketball team. This was a preview of what was to come in his successful basketball career later on in life.

Steph's high school years were marked by lots of growth and recognition. He led his school basketball team to multiple conference titles and state playoff appearances.

One game at a time, one season at a time, Steph built his reputation. He was always learning and studying those around him.

He became well-known for being able to read the court and make fast decisions - such as making the right pass at the right time, waiting for the right moment to launch the perfect shot, or helping the right teammate get open.

This drew the attention of college scouts from across the entire country.

Although Steph had some advantages of his upbringing - his sporting family, involvement in basketball, and ability to play often - his journey still had many obstacles. There was some pressure to live up to his father's legacy: *"Since his dad was a successful basketball player, shouldn't his son be one, too?"*.

Some people were also skeptical of Steph's ability to succeed at the professional level, mostly due to his smaller size.

But Steph's response to these challenges was always the same: hard work, determination, confidence, and a strong belief in what he could do on the court.

Steph's early years were a blend of family support, studying, and a deep love for basketball. With this, he became a great athlete, as well as a strong leader and someone who could think very clearly on the basketball court.

His journey helped him grow from a young boy in Charlotte to a college basketball sensation... and it showed what can be done with the right support, hard work, and going after your dreams.

Chapter 3: Sharpening Skills: From Playground to Playmaker

"Every time I rise up to shoot, I have confidence that I'm going to make it." - Stephen Curry

Stephen Curry's arrival at Davidson College was the start of a special chapter in his basketball career. At Davidson, a smaller school known more for academics than athletics, Steph found the perfect place to showcase his talents to those who doubted him.

When Steph first stepped onto the Davidson campus, he was mostly unknown outside of basketball circles. Even though he had very impressive high school achievements, bigger college programs had overlooked him, as they had some doubts about him.

This was mostly due to his smaller size and physical strength. Davidson offered him the chance to play significant minutes and also be a team leader—a challenge he was ready and excited to accept.

Under the guidance of Coach Bob McKillop, Steph quickly adapted to the college game's fast pace and more physical style. His freshman (first) year was impressive, but it was his sophomore (second) season that truly put him on the map and made him well-known in college basketball.

That year, Steph led Davidson on a successful run through the NCAA tournament, capturing the hearts of basketball fans nationwide.

His performances in these games—especially his ability to hit crucial shots and make game-changing plays—highlighted his exceptional shooting skills and his sharp basketball mind.

Steph also knew the importance of keeping up with his studies. Off the court, Steph was just as disciplined and committed as he was on the basketball court. He was a dedicated student, known among other students and his professors, for his politeness and humility. His time at Davidson wasn't just about developing as a player; it was about growing as a person.

The values of teamwork, leadership, and being an excellent student, were all very important to his experience at the college.

Steph's college career was not just successful in terms of statistics and awards; it changed who he was. He set many school and conference records, including points in a season and career three-pointers, which are still celebrated at Davidson.

More importantly, he proved that with hard work and determination, it was possible to achieve great things, no matter where you start, or how small you might be.

By the end of his time at Davidson, Steph had not only secured his place as one of college basketball's biggest stars, but he had also laid the foundation for his future success in the NBA.

His journey through Davidson showed that the right environment and support could help talent flourish, even in the most unexpected places.

Chapter 4: Dreams to Draft: Stephen's Leap to the NBA

"I can get better. I haven't reached my ceiling yet on how well I can shoot the basketball."
- Stephen Curry

Steph Curry's transition from a college sensation at Davidson, to a rookie (first-year) in the NBA, marked both the beginning of his professional basketball career and a new chapter for the NBA as he would change the game forever.

Drafted by the Golden State Warriors in 2009 as the seventh overall pick, Steph entered the NBA with high expectations - and a lot to prove.

Did you know?

WHAT IS THE NBA DRAFT?

The NBA Draft is an important yearly event where basketball teams from the National Basketball Association (NBA) choose new players to join their teams. It's like a big school pick-up game where the teams take turns choosing the players they think are the best.

Each team gets a chance to pick young players who are just starting out from college, or arrive to play in the NBA from different countries around the world.

It's a very exciting day for the players - they find out which team they will start their professional basketball careers with, and it's also exciting for the teams because they get to add new talent to help them win more games.

He had done very well in college, and - as we've already seen - was raised in a sporting family with a professional-basketball-playing dad. When he was drafted into the NBA, people expected a lot from him.

The transition was challenging, as the NBA was much more physical and competitive than he was used to in college basketball. It was a big step up. But Steph's work ethic and dedication to improving his game paid off, as he quickly adapted to the higher level of play in the NBA.

In his rookie season, Stephen made an impact on the Warriors straight away, showcasing his sharp shooting and playmaking skills.

He finished the season with impressive statistics - he averaged over 17 points per game, which earned him a spot on the NBA All-Rookie First Team.

This early success was a clear sign that Stephen was not 'just another rookie'; he was a rising star with the potential to shape the future of basketball.

Did you know?

ALL-ROOKIE TEAMS

The NBA's All-Rookie First Team is a super-team, created each year to celebrate the best new basketball players in the NBA. Imagine if at the end of the school year, your teachers picked the best new students in each subject and made a list to say "Great job!" That's what the NBA does with basketball players who are playing their very first year in the league. They choose the five most outstanding rookie players, and this is called the All-Rookie Team.

Off the court, Steph's rookie year was also a time of big personal growth. Moving to a new city (San Francisco) and starting his professional career, he embraced the extra responsibilities that came with being an NBA player. He became involved in community activities, giving back to society, and using his fame to help others.

Even though he had early success in the NBA, his first years weren't without challenges.

He suffered many injury setbacks, which tested his resilience and determination: would he push through with his rehab, keep his mind sharp, and recover? Or would he give up?

As we know by now: Steph had learned to be strong in the face of challenges. Instead of letting injuries get his career off track, he focused on recovery and strengthening his body, which eventually helped him return to the court stronger than ever before.

Did you know?

FAMILY TIES

Steph's younger brother, Seth Curry, also plays in the NBA. The Curry brothers are known for their deep bond and shared love of basketball. They're often seen cheering for each other during games.

Their father, Dell Curry, played in the NBA, and the brothers spent much of their childhood in gyms and stadiums. They were always close, and that closeness centered around their shared love for basketball.

Even though now they play for different teams, they continue to support each other's careers, often seen attending each other's games.

With his special shooting skills, Steph was a dangerous opponent on the court. Teams had to start planning for how to stop him - and often, this was impossible.

He would continue to improve his skills throughout his career, but even in these early stages: he was starting to change how basketball was played.

Chapter 5: The Golden Touch: Curry's Championship Era

"I've never been afraid of big moments. I get butterflies... I get nervous and anxious, but I think those are all good signs that I'm ready for the moment." - Stephen Curry

As Steph Curry moved into the prime of his NBA career, he continued to impress with individual performances, and also led the Warriors to a period of success they had never seen in the past.

This chapter highlights the pinnacle of his career (so far), with championship victories and individual achievements that established his influence on the sport.

Did you know?

WHAT DOES STEPH DO FOR FUN?

HISTORIAN

Curry has a keen interest in American history and often visits historical sites and museums during his travels. He thinks that understanding the past is key to making sense of where we are now, and how to improve in the future.

Steph often shares his insights in interviews and on social media, as he believes education is so important.

DANCE MOVES

Curry is known for his celebratory dance moves on the court. He's often dancing after making a big shot, before the game to get excited, or with his teammates just for fun and to relax.

These spontaneous dances are a fan favorite and show his joyful approach to the game.

FASHION FORWARD

Known for his sharp dress sense, Curry has a keen interest in fashion.

He often works with designers for the outfits he wears on game day, and has talked about an interest in launching his own clothing line later in life.

SOCIAL MEDIA SAVVY

Stephen Curry is highly active on social media, where he shares insights into his training routines, family life, and behind-the-scenes action. His Instagram and Twitter accounts are a hit with fans - they like his openness and authenticity.

BEACH LOVER

When he's not playing basketball, Curry loves to spend time at the beach. Surfing is one of his favorite activities, and he often takes family vacations to seaside destinations.

The 2014-2015 NBA season was a turning point for Steph and the Warriors. They had the guidance of new head coach Steve Kerr. Kerr was a successful player (and shooter) in the 1990s and 2000s, and played alongside Michael Jordan and Scottie Pippen in several championship teams as a player. He had now moved into the next phase of his career: a coach.

Steve Kerr - Warriors Head Coach

Steph's playing style — supported by fast ball movement and long-range shooting — became the team's cornerstone - one of their most important assets of all.

That season, his extraordinary skills and leadership led the Warriors to their first NBA championship in 40 years, and Stephen earned his first MVP (Most Valuable Player) award, highlighting his status as one of the league's best players.

The following years saw the Warriors dominate the NBA, with Steph playing a crucial role.

In the 2015-2016 season, he achieved something truly historic: he became the first player ever to be unanimously voted the NBA Most Valuable Player.

This means that every single person who voted for the MVP award, voted for Steph. This had never happened before in the history of the NBA. His record-breaking 402 three-pointers that season broke the previous records and redefined what seemed possible in basketball.

Steph's impact was not just in scoring and championships.

His skills, attitude, popularity, and playing style, all changed how basketball was played globally.

His ability to shoot from long distance, and his unselfish play, inspired a new generation of players and teams to play in a similar style, emphasizing skill and precision over traditional play.

Did you know?

MEET THE SPLASH BRIGADE!

The Warriors had a super team during their championship years, sometimes called the "Splash Brigade."
This team included five amazing players who were often unstoppable when they were all on the court at the same time: Stephen Curry, Klay Thompson, Kevin Durant ("KD"), Draymond Green, and Andre Iguodala.

They were so good together that other teams found it really tough to play against them. The "Splash Brigade" was famous because they could score a lot of points quickly, especially from beyond the three-point line, and they played great defense too.

Steph, Klay, and KD were all incredible at shooting three-pointers. This meant that the other team found it very difficult to stop them from scoring.

This often left other areas open for the Warriors to score even more. Draymond and Andre excelled at stopping the other team from scoring, and were also great passers, which made the Warriors tough to beat.

The "Splash Brigade" helped the Warriors win two NBA Championships in 2017 and 2018 because they played basketball in a new and exciting way. They ran fast, passed the ball to whoever was open, and scored big from long distance. Their style of play changed how other teams in the NBA played basketball too, making the game more about quick moves and long shots.

They weren't just a team; they were like basketball superheroes - they changed the game!

Off the court, Steph continued to shine as well. His involvement in community projects, his approach to putting family first, and his humble attitude (even with all his success), made him a role model for many.

His influence extended beyond basketball, affecting community programs, youth sports, and education programs.

Steph's journey through these championship years also had many challenges. Injuries and intense competition (especially from the Cleveland Cavaliers and LeBron James) tested him, but he was always able to rise to the occasion - especially during important playoff games.

His performances, particularly in clutch moments, solidified his reputation as a player who thrives under pressure.

Steph will not only be remembered as a great basketball player. He'll also be remembered as someone who changed the game.

And as someone who made a positive impact on those around him by contributing to society.

His path from an unknown, smaller college player, to an elite professional basketball player shows what can be done with hard work, focus, and playing with joy.

He's inspired millions with his play, while still remaining humble and focusing on his team, family, and doing what he can to make the world a better place, even outside of basketball.

Chapter 6: "More Than a Player: Stephen Off the Court"

"I try and use every game as an opportunity to witness" - Stephen Curry

Steph's influence goes further than his breathtaking performances on the basketball court. He makes a positive impact in many other areas - with his community involvement, family life, and business ventures.

Next, we'll learn about aspects of Stephen's life that show his character and values off the court.

He's not only a superstar athlete. Steph is also a dedicated family man, married to Ayesha Curry, a chef and entrepreneur. He balances his career with a robust family life.

The couple has three kids, and Stephen is known for being an active and engaged father. His family often features in his public appearances.

Did you know?

STEPH: MAN OF MANY INTERESTS

GOLF WHIZ

Aside from basketball, Curry is a keen golfer and has participated in several celebrity golf tournaments. His passion for golf has been showcased in charity events, where he even competes against professional golfers!

CAR COLLECTOR

Curry has a keen interest in cars and owns a collection that includes several high-end models. His garage features everything from sporty convertibles to luxury SUVs. He loves both style and speed!

BOOKWORM

Off the court, Curry is an avid reader and often reads books on leadership and psychology. This helps him improve his mental game and leadership skills. Reading helps him relax and stay focused during the season.

In the community, his impact runs deep. He and his wife founded the "Eat. Learn. Play." foundation to help underprivileged kids have better access to food, education, and sports.

This is one way Steph uses his fame and status to make a difference. Through his foundation, he's launched numerous programs that teach people about food and nutrition, and create safe places for kids to play and to learn.

He's also a big supporter of social issues. He has used his fame and social media to speak out on matters such as equality, community safety, and social justice. This has helped make him a role model for adults, aspiring athletes, and young people.

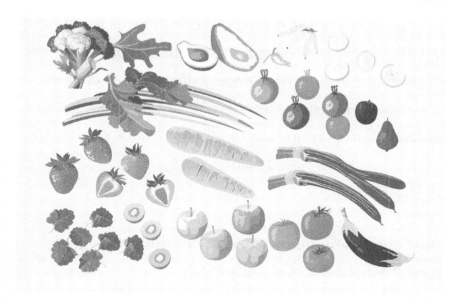

Did you know?

CHARITABLE CHEF

Curry uses his cooking skills for good causes. He has hosted several cooking events to raise money for community service programs, combining his love for food and helping others. He has organized and participated in several charity cooking events where he cooks and serves meals.

The money raised from these events goes towards community service programs, including those that feed people who don't have enough food. These cooking events not only showcase his cooking skills, but also his commitment to giving back to the community in creative and helpful ways.

What about his influence overseas? Stephen's international influence is also huge.

He has been involved in basketball development programs around the world, helping to spread the game of basketball.

He's participated in tours and camps in Asia and Europe, which has helped increase basketball's popularity and inspired countless young players.

Steph's legacy off the court is as impactful as his sporting achievements. He shows just how athletes can use their fame for positive change - making him not just a standout athlete, but also a representative for change who helps others.

Did you know?

STEPH OUTSIDE OF BASKETBALL

TECH ENTHUSIAST

An avid tech enthusiast, Curry is interested in the latest gadgets and often uses cutting-edge technology to improve his training and recovery.

For his physical recovery, he sometimes uses advanced tech like cryotherapy chambers, which help reduce muscle inflammation and speed up recovery time. They do this by exposing the body to very cold temperatures, then naturally warming up again. He also uses wearables that monitor his physical condition and provide information to help him perform better on game days.

Beyond personal use, Steph is involved in the tech world through investments. He has invested in tech startups that improve sports performance, and also make games more exciting for fans - a virtual reality sports training program (where athletes can pretend they're in a game-like situation without getting tired).

Steph also invested in a mobile app that helps fans get seat upgrades and watch instant replays on their phones, bringing them closer to the game.

Steph's use and interest in technology show how he believes innovation is really important. Both in transforming sports, helping athletes become better, and making sports more exciting and engaging for fans, too.

COMMUNITY LEADER

Steph is deeply involved in community service in the Bay Area, where he lives. He runs education and basketball camps for kids who might not be able to afford to join sports programs, aiming to inspire and motivate them through sports.

At these camps, kids learn to play basketball, work as a team, and gain confidence. Steph also helps schools in the Bay Area by giving them books and computers, making it easier for kids to learn and do their homework. Every year, Steph and his family also host a fun run, where people come to run and play, and the money they raise goes to help kids eat healthy meals at school.

He wants to make the world a better place, just like superheroes do in stories. He uses his fame to encourage others to help too - showing that everyone can do something to make a difference.

ENVIRONMENTALIST

Curry is passionate about the environment, and looking after our planet. He's an active supporter of environmental conservation. How does he do this? He talks to people about using less plastic, which can hurt animals and the earth. Steph tries to show how to be more sustainable - how we can reuse everyday things instead of throwing them away. And, he works with organizations that plant trees in cities and towns to make them greener and cleaner.

Just like you might plant a seed in a garden, he helps plant lots of trees! Sometimes, he joins in on beach clean-ups, where he and others pick up trash from the beach so it's nicer for everyone and safer for sea animals.

Beyond the Arc: Lessons from a Legend

As we've learned, Steph's story is not just about basketball. It's about believing in yourself, working hard, and the incredible things you can do when you stay positive.

From backyard hoops in Charlotte to the bright lights of the NBA, Stephen Curry has shown that greatness is not just about talent. It's about putting in the work, being dedicated, and committing to your dreams.

Sometimes obstacles, injuries, or doubts might come up along the way - this is normal. Even Steph Curry had them!

But from Steph, we learn that if you keep going, keep practicing, and keep doing good in the world - great things happen.

His story teaches us that success comes from more than just what you can do on the court; it's about who you are as a person, and how you impact those around you.

What else should we remember from Steph's journey?

- **Perseverance.** Even though many people had doubts about his basketball future due to his smaller size, Steph reminds us that you don't have to be the biggest or the strongest to succeed. He became one of the fastest, most skilled, best shooters on the planet. He didn't need to be super tall!

- **Commitment.** His commitment to practice, putting in the work, and constant improvement teaches us not to just settle for 'good enough.'

- **Having fun.** Steph's always dancing. Smiling. Laughing. Joking with teammates. Giving away shoes to his fans. His joyous approach to basketball shows that success is not just about winning - but also about enjoying what you do.

Off the court, Steph's dedication to his family, his community, and making a positive impact sets an example for all of us. His work with children's education and nutrition shows how we can all use our talents to make a difference.

Thank you for joining us on this exploration of Stephen Curry's life. We hope you are inspired by his story, and motivated by the great things he's been able to achieve with hard work.

Just like Steph, you can set goals, work hard, and have a lot of fun. No dream is too small, and no challenge is too big if you have faith in yourself and are ready to put in the effort.

Don't forget the trivia section and timeline coming up next - test your knowledge, impress your friends and family, and see who knows the most about Steph!

Thanks for reading.

Stephen Curry Trivia Challenge

Test your knowledge with these 30 trivia questions about Stephen Curry! Choose the correct answer from the options provided for each question.

Many of these are contained in this book.

Some aren't - so you might know them already, or you might learn something new.

Test yourself, test your family, and try these out on your friends to find out who is the biggest Stephen Curry Expert!

The answers are at the end.

1. Which college did Steph Curry attend?

A) UCLA

B) Davidson

C) Duke

2. In what year did Steph win his first NBA championship?

A) 2014

B) 2015

C) 2016

3. How many NBA Most Valuable Player (MVP) Awards has Stephen Curry won?

A) One

B) Two

C) Three

4. Which of these is a charity initiative started by Stephen Curry?

A) Eat. Learn. Play.

B) Play. Work. Grow.

C) Learn. Work. Build.

5. Steph is known for his skills in which other sport?

A) Golf

B) Tennis

C) Soccer

6. What is Stephen Curry's wife's name?

A) Alicia

B) Ayesha

C) Amber

7. Which is Steph's team in the NBA?

A) Los Angeles Lakers

B) Golden State Warriors

C) New York Knicks

8. What unique record did Steph set during the 2015-2016 NBA season?

A) Most three-pointers in a playoff game

B) Most three-pointers in a season

C) Highest free throw percentage in a season

9. Steph Curry has a sibling who also plays in the NBA. What is his brother's name?

A) Seth

B) Shawn

C) Sam

10. What is one of Stephen Curry's hobbies outside of basketball?

A) Painting

B) Cooking

C) Dancing

11. In which year was Stephen Curry unanimously chosen as the MVP?

A) 2014

B) 2015

C) 2016

12. What is Stephen Curry's favorite pre-game snack?

A) Sushi

B) Popcorn

C) Pizza

13. Which award show did Steph host?

A) The Grammys

B) The ESPYs

C) The Oscars

14. Curry is known for celebrating with what type of dance?

A) Breakdance

B) Shimmy

C) Salsa

15. How many children does Steph have?

A) One

B) Two

C) Three

16. What number does Curry wear for the Golden State Warriors?

A) 30

B) 23

C) 11

17. What type of business does Stephen Curry's wife run?

A) A clothing boutique

B) A bookstore

C) A restaurant

18. Which type of pet does the Curry family own?

A) Cat

B) Dog

C) Parrot

19.Steph has set records for shooting from which part of the court?

A) Free throw line

B) Mid-court

C) Beyond the three-point line

20. What does Stephen Curry often do to connect with fans?

A) Give away sneakers

B) Write personal letters

C) Host video game sessions

21. Stephen's passion for which topic has influenced his charity work?

A) Environmental conservation

B) Education

C) Animal rights

22. What major injury did Curry overcome early in his career?

A) Knee injury

B) Ankle injury

C) Shoulder injury

23. Steph was the first player to be unanimously elected MVP in which season?

A) 2014-2015

B) 2015-2016

C) 2016-2017

24. Which luxury item is Stephen known to collect?

A) Watches

B) Cars

C) Sunglasses

25. Which college award did Steph Curry win?

A) Heisman Trophy

B) Naismith College Player of the Year

C) Wooden Award

26. Which international competitions has Steph participated in?

A) FIBA World Cup

B) Olympic Games

C) Both A and B

27. What is Steph's favorite type of movie?

A) Comedy

B) Action

C) Horror

28. What unique hobby does Steph share with his children?

A) Technology and gadgets

B) Kite flying

C) Stamp collecting

29. Which social media platform does Steph use most actively?

A) Instagram

B) Facebook

C) Twitter

30. What college did Steph's father, Dell Curry, attend?

A) Virginia Tech

B) North Carolina

C) UCLA

Answers

1. B - Davidson. Steph attended Davidson College from 2006 to 2009, where he made a big impact on college basketball , even though it was a small college.

2. B - 2015. Steph won his first NBA championship in 2015 with the Golden State Warriors, who defeated the Cleveland Cavaliers in the finals.

3. B - Two. Steph has been awarded the NBA Most Valuable Player (MVP) title twice, first in 2015 and then making history with a unanimous win in 2016.

4. A - Eat. Learn. Play. Steph and his wife Ayesha established the "Eat. Learn. Play." foundation to provide kids with access to nutritious food, quality education, and sports.

5. A - Golf. Apart from basketball, Steph is passionate about golf and participates in celebrity golf tournaments. He has quite a talent for the sport!

6. B - Ayesha. Ayesha Curry, Steph's wife, is a well-known culinary figure and author. They have been married since 2011 and have three kids.

7. B - Golden State Warriors. Since being drafted in 2009, Steph has played for the Golden State Warriors, making a huge impact on their successes as a team.

8. B - Most three-pointers in a season. In the 2015-2016 NBA season, Steph broke the record for the most three-pointers in a single season with 402, surpassing the previous record of 286, set by himself.

9. A - Seth. Steph's brother, Seth Curry, is also an NBA player. The two share a close bond and a love for basketball.

10. B - Cooking. Steph enjoys cooking and often takes the lead in preparing meals at home, sharing this hobby with his family.

11. C - 2016. Steph was the first-ever unanimous MVP in the NBA in 2016. This means everybody who voted, thought he should be the winner. (Usually, it's a mix of players). This is a testament to his extraordinary performance in that season!

12. B - Popcorn. Steph is famously a big fan of popcorn, often critiquing different NBA arenas based on the quality of their popcorn.

13. B - The ESPYs. Steph hosted the ESPY Awards in 2021, showcasing his versatility and charm outside the basketball court. "ESPY Award" is short for Excellence in Sports Performance Yearly Award. These honors recognize individual and team achievements in sports for that year.

14. B - Shimmy. Known for his shimmy dance on the court, Steph often celebrates his successful shots with this joyful little dance.

15. C - Three. Steph and Ayesha have three children, and family life is central to his off-court identity.

16. A - 30. Steph wears the jersey number 30. Why? To reflect and continue on his dad's professional career - 30 is the same number his dad, Dell Curry, wore on the court.

17. C - Restaurant. Ayesha owns a restaurant, and Steph supports her business ventures, often getting involved with the promotion of the restaurant.

18. B - Dog. The Curry family includes a dog. Steph and his family love pets and animals!

"Rookie", the goldendoodle.

19. C - Beyond the three-point line. Steph has changed the game of basketball with his ability to consistently make shots from well beyond the three-point line.

20. A - Give away sneakers. After many games, Steph gives his game-worn sneakers to young fans, a gesture that has become well-known among his followers.

21. B - Education. Through his foundation, Steph prioritizes education, funding programs that give better learning opportunities for underprivileged kids. These kids might not otherwise have access to a good education, so the program has a big impact!

22. B - Ankle injury. Steph overcame significant ankle injuries early in his career. He had to work hard to get back to normal, but this led to him becoming stronger, and ultimately didn't derail his career.

23. B - 2015-2016. Steph's 2015-2016 season was historic, earning him the first unanimous MVP award in NBA history. This means he got ALL the

votes for the MVP. Something that had never happened up until that point.

24. B - Cars. A car enthusiast, Steph enjoys collecting and driving various high-performance cars.

25. B - Naismith College Player of the Year. At Davidson, Steph was honored as the Naismith College Player of the Year, highlighting his dominance in college basketball.

26. A - FIBA World Cup. Steph represented the United States in international basketball at the FIBA World Cup, showing his skills on a global stage. He had a big hand in the team's success in winning gold medals in 2010 and 2014.

27. A - Comedy. Steph enjoys comedy movies and shows; he often mentions that watching them is one of his favorite ways to relax and unwind after games or during the off-season.

28. A - Technology. Steph is a big tech enthusiast! He likes to try out the latest gadgets and tech trends.

This is both for fun, during his downtime, and for his training and recovery.

29. A - Instagram. Steph is very active on Instagram, where he shares snippets of his personal life, professional highlights, and moments from his training sessions, connecting with millions of fans worldwide.

30. A - Virginia Tech. While Steph attended Davidson College, his father, Dell Curry, played his college basketball at Virginia Tech, making it a significant part of the family's athletic legacy.

Curry's Climb: Rise of a Sharpshooter

Here's a timeline of some of the most iconic, important and influential milestones in Steph Curry's life (so far!):

- **March 14, 1988:** Stephen Curry is born in Akron, Ohio.

- **2006:** Steph enters Davidson College, where he quickly becomes a standout player for his college team, the Davidson Wildcats.

- **March 21, 2008:** Leads Davidson to the Elite Eight (the last eight teams in the tournament of the 68 who started) in the NCAA Tournament, scoring 40 points against Gonzaga in the first round.

- **June 25, 2009:** Drafted 7th by the Golden State Warriors in the NBA Draft.

- **2010:** Named to the NBA All-Rookie First Team after an excellent first season, averaging 17.5 points, 5.9 assists, and 4.5 rebounds per game.

- **February 27, 2013:** Breaks the NBA single-season record for three-pointers made, finishing the season with 272, surpassing Ray Allen's previous record of 269 set in the 2005-2006 season.

- **May 4, 2015:** Wins his first NBA MVP Award, leading the NBA in steals per game and free throw percentage, and ranking second in points per game with 23.8.

- **June 16, 2015:** Leads the Warriors to their first NBA Championship in 40 years by defeating the Cleveland Cavaliers in six games. Steph averaged 26.0 points, 6.3 assists and 5.2 rebounds in 6 games.

- **May 10, 2016:** Becomes the first unanimous MVP in NBA history, receiving all 131 first-place votes and breaking his own record with 402 three-pointers in the regular season.

- **June 12, 2017:** Wins his second NBA Championship as the Warriors defeat the Cleveland Cavaliers in five games. This time he averaged 26.8 points, 9.4 assists and 8.0 rebounds in 5 games.

- **June 8, 2018:** Wins his third NBA Championship with the Warriors completing a sweep of the Cleveland Cavaliers in the Finals. Steph averaged 27.5 points, 6.8 assists and 6.0 rebounds in the 4 games.

- **2019:** The Warriors move to the Chase Center in San Francisco from Oracle Arena in Oakland.

- **April 13, 2019:** Breaks the all-time Warriors scoring record previously held by Wilt Chamberlain, with his 17,784th point. He did this with a huge game: 53 points in the Warriors' 116-107 win over the Nuggets, including 10 3-pointers.

- **March 5, 2020:** Launches the "Eat. Learn. Play." foundation to support children's health, education, and access to sports.

- **December 14, 2021:** Breaks the NBA record for career three-pointers made during a game against the New York Knicks at Madison Square Garden, surpassing Ray Allen's career total of 2,973. This historic event, witnessed by shooting greats Ray Allen, Reggie Miller and others, further cements Curry's legacy as one of the greatest shooters in basketball history.

- **February 20, 2022:** on the NBA All-Star Game Kobe Bryant Most Valuable Player Award. He scored 50 points, 48 of which came from a record-setting 16 3-pointers. This was a new record for 3-pointers in an All-Star game.

- **June 16, 2022:** Wins his fourth NBA Championship and is named NBA Finals MVP. He averaged 31.2 points, 6.0 rebounds and 5.0 assists in 6 games, leading the series in scoring and helping the Warriors defeat the Boston Celtics in six games.

- **April 25, 2024:** Curry receives the 2023–24 NBA Clutch Player of the Year Award. This award goes to the player who performed best under pressure and made important, winning plays during close games. This often includes great passes, exceptional defense, or game-winning buzzer beaters. Steph won this award because he hit several game-winners, and helped his team to win many times in the final moments of several close games.

Claim Your Free Bonus Coloring Book

There's a free bonus coloring book download waiting for you, as a thank you for picking up this book. We think you'll like it.

Just scan the QR code below or visit *ColorCraftBooks.com/colorcraft-bonus*.

Kids: Make sure to ask a parent first!

Scan to get your free coloring book download.

Thanks for reading.

Would you help us with a review?

If you enjoyed the book, we'd be so grateful you could help us out by leaving a review on Amazon (even a super short one!). Reviews help us so much - in spreading the word, in helping others decide if the book is right for them, and as feedback for our team.

If you'd like to give us any suggestions, need help with something, or to find more books like this, please visit us at ColorCraftBooks.com.

Thank you

Thank you so much for picking up *All About Steph Curry*. We really hope you enjoyed it, and learned a lot about this extraordinary athlete.

Thanks again,

The Color Craft team

Made in the USA
Las Vegas, NV
22 December 2024

15245081R00049